WRITING MY PAIN

WRITING MY PAIN

**"With pain comes healing
With healing come strength"**

By: Christopher Bonner

WRITING MY PAIN

iUniverse books may be ordered through booksellers or by contacting:

iUniverse
1663 Liberty Drive
Bloomington, IN 47403
www.iuniverse.com
1-800-Authors (1-800-288-4677)

Because of the dynamic nature of the Internet, any web addresses or links contained in this book may have changed since publication and may no longer be valid. The views expressed in this work are solely those of the author and do not necessarily reflect the views of the publisher, and the publisher hereby disclaims any responsibility for them.

Any people depicted in stock imagery provided by Thinkstock are models, and such images are being used for illustrative purposes only. Certain stock imagery © Thinkstock.

ISBN: 978-1-5320-2073-5 (sc)
ISBN: 978-1-5320-2074-2 (e)

Print information available on the last page.

iUniverse rev. date: 04/10/2017

Chapter 1

Me Against The World

Chapter 2

<u>Love Don't Cost A Thing</u>

Chapter 3

Life Lessons

Chapter 1 – Me Against The World

Unarmed And Dangerous

So much anger aimed at us
There is no one around to blame or trust
No helping hand to fight for us
Another man has to bite the dust
Took a bite of crime
Before teething
This is why people of my kind
Dying for no reason
Tis the season
For treason
Every man created equal
But are they equally treated
Spare me the sequel
Before I get peacefully heated
Calm before the storm
Fire will dry the rain
Along with our tears
What shall we do with the pain
Let it marinate
Or retaliate
Deprived our innocence
With no attempt to validate
We are guilty
Of being young, black, and filthy

Them bewildered
Because I paint the perfect picture
No filter
Draining the watered down propaganda
To be brutally honest
Let us have our moment
That is usually tarnished
Let us take a moment of silence
To heal the womb
They display the body
However, conceal the tomb
Now can you see what we are up against
We must kill them with kindness
To rebuild them with confidence

Feel Free

All because I am mad
I do not have the right to smile
So when I am happy
There is no way I can mug
Another proud dread head
Labeled as a thug
An addiction begins with a choice
Some choose to love
Bad habits ruin dreams
Most worse than drugs
So feel free to be
Who you want to be
Not a wanna be
Why would you want to be like somebody
Who is trying to be somebody else
That is like trying help somebody
That is not trying to help them self
So feel free to open up for isolation
Instead of feeling trapped in an imitation
Break the cycle
Build a bridge to a new land
Dead men walking in a broken system
It is time for a new plan
So feel free to be scared of starting over

Because revenge is going backwards
Often confused with closure
Keep your composure
Fear what they do not understand
Claims to honor man
With no effort to comprehend
So feel free to be different
Feel free to be ashamed
Because the ones that hide their feelings
Usually hide the blame
Why practice
When you feel perfect
Why sellout
When you know it is not worth it
Be patient
Feel free to wait your turn
Because the ones that rush pass their mistakes
Probably will never learn

Backstabbers

Can you look into the eyes
Of the guys
That reside on the other side
The backside
A bullseye on the spine
As they approach from behind
No feelings
Nor thoughts in their mind
Wonder if they have a heart
If so
Would have sense this coming from the start
Throwing daggers like darts
Backstabbing in the dark
However, in the light
They seem to lose sight
Of everything we have been through
Threw it all away like tissue
No magazines here
How was I suppose to know we had an issue
Subscriptions on the final page
Right where you applied the blade
You thrive in shame
Throughout the shade
Grooming others' accolades

No aftershave
Razors without the stage
Behind the scenes
Schemes out the cage
Red ink bleed out with rage
Plenty pressure on this precious womb
No budget to invest in tombs
Just another swordsman that never felt the doom
Just another witch that never swept her broom
Please do not assume
Jesus whelp for whom
Those who pump the heat
Can't even adjust the fumes

Twist The Cap Back

I am boiling hot
You need more than an iceberg to get me froze
So much anger bottled up
Down flat and I still explode
One of a kind
You need more than a brand to get me sold
Real recognize real
Lacking fizz will get you exposed
With my back concealed
Still managed to pop my top
When you cracked the seal
Time to have that pep talk
With this Pepsi
My pep rallied
No need to prep
Born ready
Since the distillery
Palms heavy
Special delivery
For spectating my history
Speculations ineligible
Bold statements are edibles
All I have is my word and my spectacles
So twist my cap back
And let me complete my schedule

Sacrifice

What are you willing to give up to gain
It depends on your motivational aim
Exchange pleasure for pain
That is the name
Of the game
This is not something you play with
More like pay with
Lay with
And stay with
Through my eyes
Likewise
You can forgive and forget
But this will last for a lifetime
I can put my life on it
Priceless
Doesn't have a price on it
It is all a gamble
Sometimes you have to shake the dice on it
Unpredictable
Nothing like a ritual
Most don't understand
Until it gets physical
Knees scrubbing the floor
As an attempt to get spiritual

He already knows
Because the feeling is mutual
Tell me something I don't know
Show me something I know so
No response
You consider that as a low blow
I love you my child
But a weakness I won't show
Man made money
Therefore, it can't make the world spin
I made gravity
So the world could whirlwind
Rumors make y'all spin
Still no connections at bald ends
My son was a sacrifice
He died for all sins

Misunderstood

Supplied by wealth
I am fly to death
No matter the degree
It provides my health
Skeletons in my closet
Still meat no the bones
No time to roam
Killing two birds with one stone
One was thrown
While the other got wasted
Deuce with the juice
But what am I chasing
In love with competition
But whom am I facing
Feelings of first place
Forgot whom I was racing
Another no show
What shall I do with my patience
Play doctor
Surgically remove my ankles
Play possum
My feet planted proper
Your foot in a locker
Imposters buckle up

Living as you are guaranteed to wreck
Wagers on life
Is there really a need to bet
Especially when odds are against me
What is a 50/50 share
When your vision is impaired
A 20/20 stare
Foreseeable future
Steady judging from my past
I am guilty for being misunderstood
While my innocence is proven last

Die Slow

I hope that hate eats your body inside out
And you still don't die
Then chug on your blood
Until your bones go dry
I hope those
Begin to mold and decay
And pits of hell
Take a toll on your soul everyday
Constant breaking point
Where you tear every joint and ligament
Blessed with a quick recovery
Just to break and bend again
Your arch nemesis
Is your designated master
Cursed with headaches
Until your skull is fractured
Piercing pains travel down your spinal cord
Infected wombs reopened by a viral sword
Rats feeding on fallen remains
Worms squirming your brain
Maggots having a blast surfing your surface
You wishing time would fly
Dodging bullets in the matrix
Froze in the twilight zone

Clicking your heels
There's no place like home
Visions of such place
Only possible through hallucinations
Vaccines for the virus
Also known as hatred
Rejected the cure
Red roses to edit
No doc in sight
Plenty patience for your slow exit

I Deserve It

I've surpass my breaking point
To reveal my waking point
Woke up from my American Dream
Sweating at my tanking point
Rock bottom
No predator can devour this
Power couple
Singled out now I am powerless
Self made territory
Conquered by my pride
Standup guy
Counldn't even stand by my own side
Forced to crawl like the baby I am
Until my knees ache
Every breath is like fish out of water
Hooked on it like I need bait
No grace for this supper plate
Rather suffer from starvation before I suffocate
On a dinner date with death
Grim reaper the chef
Knowing he put his foot in it
Because I can't take a step
Stuck in this situation
Me and my meditation

Food for thoughts outside the box
Intimidated by my mental anticipation
Judgements are clouded
Immoral precipitation
Swimming with my nose above water
Having growth to embrace it
With this pen I sin with the hands of time
At the end, I have to face it

Better Late Than Never

It is better to be late than never
Tell that to the ones that left my heart severed
Dumbfounded
No matter how clever
So much salt in the game
The chef cannot find the pepper
It takes two to tango
Well I was a lonely sad hatch
Love is so beautiful
Somebody sold me a bad batch
I bought the lies
And stole the time
Daylight savings in autumn
Yet I still fell behind
Back on my feet
And tried again
You fought truth
Therefore, I lied again
When did forever turn into a century
When did a lifetime reduce to a decade
I guess love is not eternal
At my worst on your best days
Better hours coming soon
I am midnight

When you are noon
Generate sunshine
While I reflect like the moon
On this little light of mine
Has put me in a bind
Availability restricted
Nevertheless, I will be there right on time

Back Like I Never Left

Gone with the wind
No need to wipe the dust off
Moneymaking machine
My green keep the rust off
Did not mean to rush off
No average speed to want more
A meeting with the kings of Mount Rushmore
That destination at a distance
Yet I will be back in an instance
Like when the rivers flow
With no resistance
You could be equipped with the proper equipment
Cannot stop my drive
Because I am relentless
Fueled by resentment
Abandonment in my rear view
As I am seated on the pedal
Brakes blanketed by mildew
Heated like a kettle
Steamed up just to shield you
Protection from a far
While my presence in a car
Godspeed is a gift
Give you a lift to the star

Can you see me now
Or still trying to bring me down
Well I am back in the flesh
Watch me spread like a sea of clouds
Reported as foggy
Evaluated as all me
Cycle like the waves of the oceans
Yet I am not salty
Haunted by the bitter taste
Shocked me on every step
Start fronting when I am right
That is why I am back like I never left

Eyes Wide Shut

Tell me
What do you think of a guy
That makes up his mind
In a blink of an eye
Head manifested in intestines
Still no scent of the signs
Lacks the sense to signify
A significant other
Crossing sensitive lines
Dignify the finish
Continuously slipping the mind
Perspective diminishing now
Found in a space
With no dimensions around
Darkness rises
And falls
Darts pitched at the spotlight
In awe
Relief from disbelief
He is oblivious as leaf
Who has forgotten his feet
Dragging a jagged queen
Directing pageant scenes
Maybelline for cameras

Need permission
For self recognition
Suspended suspensions
No bounce for suspicion
Provoke droughts for attention
Promote doubt as if it is religious
Out of sight
Out of mind
The power of superstition

Skeletons In The Closet

Graveyard as a wardrobe
Groundbreaking accessories
Arisen from treachery
Shade shines with legacies
Stained for centuries
Smoke fades with memories
Tombstone headboards
A two toned landlord
Working that maroon dress
Eggs in a cocoon nest
Subdued stress
Butterfly effect
A catastrophic mess
Danger on a hanger
Left high and dry
Fit for dipping
Why the tie
Wise guy in disguise
What do I have to hide
Skulls in my shoeboxes
Apparel of a new hostage
Chest plate a freezer
Will thaw for true knowledge
More than books on the shelf

Dirty dentals to chew college
Graduated with a bone to pick
Took a grudge overboard
To show ownership
King me
I own the the crypt
Keys please
I drove the ship
The same one I will not go down with
The same one the lifeguard drowned with
Feeding off of soaked concessions
Anatomy professions
Add to me as blessings
Inanimate dressings
Behold
My casualty collection

Hurt So Good

How could something heal so bad
Hurt so good
Peeled sore scabs
Blood worth no good'
Detected defectives
Still stocked more goods
Dictated electives
High intent show good
Skirts on display
Smirks of dismay
Lost my mind
While my heart was misplaced
This place
Is no man's land
Where no man
Stands a chance
Just another chair
In advance
House broken
Another stance in my pants
Stay cutting a rug
Not familiar with the dance
Foot too loose
Created a home

Under two roofs
Boo who
Guru with the voodoo
A plethora of flames
For pleasurable pain
The painkiller
With unmeasurable range
Take me there
Click my heels
No better place
Whip the wheels
Safety second
Risk appeals
To those seeking rewards
Through the thrills

Chapter 2 – Love Don't Cost A Thing

Reflection

Look in the mirror
I see regrets and apologies
Or is that my shadow
Dark familiar shape lacking the usual qualities
No resemblance of the man that was suppose to father me
Will I ever break away
Or be eternally apart of me
It is hard to see
Rocky roads
Loved ones think they close
However, seem so far to me
Blind to my inner pain
From my brain through my arteries
No drug can ease this
No therapist wants to face this
The Supreme Court would not even case this
I guess that did not make sense
But when it comes to judgement
I am tasteless
Numb to a racist
A ticking time bomb in the matrix
So pull the plug
And let me out this mirror
I feel the end is getting nearer

Because my vision is getting clearer
No fear in me
Blurred lines
Looking too clear to me
Put me out my misery
Why would I want to make history
When the truth of past
Will eventually
Become history
Unbalanced line of symmetry
Help reflect minds on memories
False agreements got me living a mystery

Is He Here Yet?

Constantly looking out of the blinds
Going blind from all the lies
Only the truth will end this tragedy
Too young to grasp what is going through our minds
You have to feel the pain in my eyes
That is why I know you are coming back for me
Brotherly love helped me understand
There is a process to become a man
Lessons from the streets
This cannot be part of the plan
A mother's touch should be a helping hand
Without you, I am incomplete
Crying myself to sleep
Waking up to defeat
Because your return equals victory
I gain strength from your speech
Have not heard from you in weeks
Growing weak from this silent symphony
Now hip-hop is music to my ears
You can tell by the company of my peers
That this young man is going through a transition
I stand alone as I fight my fears
Need a black hole to hold my tears
Those grand memories slipping like a bad transmission

Mother cannot fix that
My brother do not chit chat
I am fed up with this mix match
Just let me know when you gone get back
Staying optimistic asking if you are here yet
Cries for help on repeat
Obviously, you do not hear that
Best actor in history
An Oscar for the deadbeat with the beer fat
Had me feeling like
Used clothes in the clearance section on Sears' rack
Now when I think of you
I guarantee it will not bring a tear back
I have built a skyscraper of pain
Architects cannot engineer that
It is a cold world
And my heart may appear black
The sun shine a bit harder when I am mad
The rain keeps my grounded when I am sad
No father for discipline when I was bad
Still the greatest motivation to be something I never had
A dad

Blood Brothers

The oldest is positioned to be the idol
The youngest viewed him as a rival
Motivation to get better
Because only one can win the title
Made for love
Built for competition
Battle to be the best
But fighting is forbidden
Maturity for the older
A so-called given
Insecurity is left for the younger
It does not matter which is which
It is fulltime security for your brother
Even if it is protection from their mother
Promise to keep the code for one another
Lie on the stand
The law is not deterring me
Our bond is forever strong
It will last for an eternity
Blood is thicker than water
Some cases that is a myth
No judgement in the court
Only if, if was a fifth
Plenty drunk on your end

Living for today and not tomorrow
Vision clearer than urine
As we flush away our sorrows
Happiness is given or taken
But never ever borrowed
One day we must part ways
That is a tough pill to swallow
Medication for weak
Motivation for the strong
Best way to test our bond
Through the time we spend alone
Same book, different pages
Same game, different stages
Half of a decade
With no sense of any changes

Brother From Another Mother

Born at a distance
Blood could not make us closer
Torn in an instance
Time heals like it suppose to
You are my holster
Protection by my side
You are my Rover
Always down to ride
With all this weight on my shoulders
Right there to keep me strong
That is why it is a fine line between family and relatives
Family is through the thick and thin
While the others are just relative
My cut is what you had better give
Need luck with the way we live
Forced to look up to each other
Well that is just the way it is
Stupid is as stupid does
Focused on the future
Speaking on how it was
Reminiscing and brainstorming

Clouds flooded with drugs
Rope-a-dope to stay afloat
Spill the curtesy jug
Every quote is a joke
Now that is brotherly love

DNA/H$_2$O

Blood may be thicker than water
But which one is the purest
One can carry a virus
While the other may cure it
Wash away my sins
And cleanse
All of the sewage
Ready to spread my wings
And raise above the influence
Because society is not my family
Ironically
Family is the foundation of society
Sunk my sanity
When I hauled their variety
Blood only makes us related
The waters we sip make us retain it
So let us learn from history
To make history
Took all those losses
To give us victory
Received all those crosses
To give them misery
It is our DNA to balance out chemistry

Apology Accepted

They say you suppose to forgive and forget
Well as soon as I forgot
They schemed up a plot
Profound prophets of the top
To press profit out of the prop
Blood money cannot be refunded
Might as well burn it
With no intentions to earn it
Fire fueled in my furnace
Flamed cheeks
Still managed to turn it
Stiffness at an all-time high
A massage parlor
Could relieve these patronized barters
Disowned your own plagiarized charter
Backstabbed
My six armored with honor
Follow my words
As I lead by example
Yet you filed a false report
Desperate attempts to last in that lost resort
Petty praying for a higher resource
As soon as you apologized
I felt buyer's remorse

War cry as I retreat with the receipt
Penalty of paying the price
You fooled me once
It is about that time I schooled you twice
Took my kindness for weakness
A square with snake eyes before I rolled your dice
No need for retaliation
This calls for a surprise celebration
To the clone who roams the hills that is filled with humiliation

Friendly Fire

Your biggest fear
You conquered and delivered it
Before I could stand clear of it
A collision course with karma
Without preparation or deliverance
I must overcome the fear of it
You get out what you put in to it
Concept legitimate
Depending on your intent for it
Benefits blown up like images
Home sick
With a thorn to pick
Hard nose
Soft-spoken suddenly shows
Exposed
When you have devoted discipline
Towards a distant man
No sense of suspicion
With hidden intentions
Simply said, "Yes sir"
No matter how absurd
Take a step back and observe
The appraisals from upward
Needing to catch up

If you telling me what you must heard
Poison spread on that bread
Appetizer for the Guinea Pig
The body is dead without a head
Flip and tell as the penny did
One for all
Or all for one
All and all
Look at what you have done
Rather be selfish than selfless
Well swim at your own risk
Shellfish

At First Sight

So easy on the eye
I find it hard to blink
If looks could kill
Unbiased scope with a winsome wink
Abducted wisdom teeth
The taste of love using lens to think
No process on impulse
Why you think we binge to drink
Views under the fruitful rum
Ripens a truthful tongue
Shaken shackles from the shallows
Breathtaking given an useful lung
Emerge with an urge
So unique
Feast your eyes upon a physique
So mystique
The buzz has the hives craving
To have pupils dilated
By pores dehydrated
Tears stored to endure being illuminated
How could one individual
Redeem rituals from residuals
Hindsight habitual

Stampedes cross seas to get visuals
Looks can be deceiving
While words are misleading
The truth hurts, yet relieving
Because seeing is believing

In The Worst Way

What type of person makes a death wish on their birthday
Me, because I want the best for you in the worst way
And they say
"Save the best for last"
Well in that case
I will never be first place
Marathon of love
Cruising at a steady pace
Rerun beloved
Bruises from a heavy race
Relapsing finish lines
After collapsing the scrimmage line
I am all-in every play
Each and every way
Wagers on my heart
Because my state of mind is on the line
Crazy for your love
Give me asylum time if you are not mine
Every since the green light
I been rolling through stop signs
Walking by faith
So our love is not blind
The lord as my witness
If loving you is wrong

I am praying for forgiveness
Given our fitness
Forbidden we worked out
Got taken for granted
When my access was denied
I grabbed this pen and panicked

Exchange

Tit for tat

There is an X for every O

We chit and chat

With stress in every code

Over this and that

Shedding flesh for pots of gold

We missed our match

When we shared a solid soul

We rock and roll

Paid paper for the scissors

We lock and load

Maintain flame throughout the blizzard

When it rains, it pours

I am insane for more

Because I love the way she lie

As she cry me a river

I float assure

On the brim of the bank

Currencies of love

Burning snow in the tank

Exhausted pipes

Have our hearts been frosted

The flame is still burning

However, cannot find where we lost it

Another necessity you can do without
It is my specialty to hold the burn within
Now every time you come in
You command an objective
Yet cannot comprehend
Why you demand like detectives
For every person I offend
That pretend to be respective
There is a couple I defend
Well it depends on perspective
I have undercut everything you overseen
Because my lips seem
To speak with a tongue from overseas
I am still your underdog
That was not overlooked
Schemed up a scene
For the show to be took
By your chosen crook
Even after closed curtains
We remain an open book

What Happened To Us

I guess
You do not find me funny anymore
You just
Keep it dry with me on any shore
Caught up in the waves
Lost in our ways
Found ourselves in a maze
Promised it was just a phase
So why
Does this feel like forever
We try
To hold on when it feels like whatever
You was gone in an instance
Spoke it into existence
I am a mute
Silence is another form of resistance
Lord knows
Life with love not hard to handle
Cards fold
I bet your hand was worth the gamble
Conversations until the sunrise
To texting until our thumps tied
Confessions told from young eyes
Speaking French until our tongues dry

We floated
On snowflakes at a new altitude
Devoted
To each other, no matter the attitude
Breakup to makeup
Mutual budget through the pay cuts
Love lacks monetary value
When it is a trip to Vegas
My title
You were my Queen of Kings
Why rival?
Enough jokers to meme the team
The defense impose the fright
Offense is suppose to strike
Tried our luck and broke the dice
My heart shattered
Now it beats like a poltergeist

Took My Kindness As A Weakness

I open my door with open arms
You treated my heart like the welcome mat
The reason why those heels give me chills
Get goosebumps from new pumps
Short temper on long days
Never been rubbed the wrong way
By the Midas touch
Still gave you my all when it was not enough
Expected laughs
You respond with a yawn
Known for going over and beyond
Opened opportunities to get under my skin
Cannot do without because she dwell within
Accessed an old womb
Ditched in a gold tomb
Always had a shovel for the finer things
You will remain that way until your final ring
This is the final round
On this battleground
So take your last bow
Class clown
The circus been out of style
Your circuit been out of wire
I cannot be your outlet

Guaranteed to let you down looking upset
Adding problems
I cannot resolve
Done going in circles
My head cannot revolve
Made me adapt
Now watch me evolve
Let you swim with the sharks
As I watch you dissolve

Heartache

My heart is not broken
It is swollen
When you love hard
You fall hard
Right on my feet
Left feeling weak
Every time my heart pumps
It leaks
More of a heart tap
No longer my heart beats
This is the hard knock life
No easy roads
So let my love pave the way
Reconstruction ease the soul

Fell

When you fall
You should get back up
Well I would not have fell
If I had backup
So when I get back up
I am not hearing the words
Just weighing the facts up
Now that I am on top
You up in my background
Bottom feeders do not know
What goes up must come back down
I fell on
I fell off
I fell in
I fell out
Love, I fell out of that too
A gift and a curse
Some spells have to half two
I must be cursed
Because every since our relationship failed
I feel I have to have you
I guess I did not know
What I had until it was gone
We fell apart

Because we failed to get along
Failed to comprehend
Had to fail just to understand
Like fighting a losing battle
Setup to fail
That never feels well
Enough tears to fill a well
And not one wish came true
Except for the lies if I was to blame you

Through Thick And Thin

I stop paying attention
Because it was not worth it
Everything I fed you
Reacted as if allergic
Expectations of being perfect
What made me deserve it
Hid behind your feelings
They finally came to the surface
Frail without balance
Side effect from an earthquake
Prolonged fall to the bottom
Impact made my earth break
I cannot function outside your gravity
Causing certified casualties
Everything you fed me
Is the source to these cavities
A smile charged by batteries
I stood on my emotions
Bit my taste buds for the calories
Extra energy stored for war
A current victim of your chamber
Eager to break the peace free
Shackled down by our anger
Communication is the key

Guarded by our conscious
Mind over matter
Lack of guidance from our compass
Keeping composure to compromise
Conciliation accomplished
You forever my accomplice

Forever Young

Of course, I want to grow wise with you
Reach new heights of maturity
I refuse to grow old with you
Using light for security
Your sight serves my needs
Our souls are Siamese
Spirits cannot raid us
Certainly
It is gone take more than surgery
To separate us
Simple system
Both approach as arbitrators
Divided we stand
United common denominators
Dynamic duo
With a binding bureau
Breaking branches to the top
Forgotten roots nevermore
Went out on a limb for your love
We venture to settle scores
Vent to petals wars
Explore what you cannot ignore
A date in Hell's Kitchen
To kick the devil's door

Back for my innocence
Because every since
The discover of imminence
Only course to compensate
Is that bypass to intimate
Exercise went sport
Prepared to perform in a critical stage
Abusing this prescription
Profession at a minimum wage
I will never foul you
Just pile out in material value
Ring the bell
Or put a ring around you
Completed pledges I vow to
Wow you
Right now you
Limitless to my willingness to arouse you

Chapter 3 – Life Lessons

Good Just Not Good Enough

I did my best
I gave it my all
With intention to rise
Still I fall
Oh, I got back up
And tried again
A second at life
And died again
Whom you know that can rest in peace
While all their efforts to succeed are decease
Of course, I learned from my mistakes
To concerned with being great
How to lose your tool clever
Embraced the hate
From those with faith
On my road to get better
They still bitter
It is a cold world
I may shake never shiver
Wearing pride as a coat
Many rather lie by the throat
Than die by that quote
It is all or nothing
No in between

Managed to find myself in the mix
No grenadine
Drunk off greed
While I am in love with this buzz
Because
Everything not all good
So I will settle for good enough

Worst Enemies

Being stuck in your ways
Will have you stuck a maze
Searching for ways
To be amazed
The truth is
You are a nuisance
When it is time to keep it tight
You are the first with a loose end
Welcome to no budgets
Thanks to your need to spend
Go broke
She will not break
Guaranteed to bend
Stretching the truth
See you lying through your two lens
Eyes wide shut
Unplugged with the tube in
Laid with the screen
Baking bread with the jewels in
Beauty is pain
An addict for bruised skin
Black eyes and red cheeks
You are looking alive for a dead beat

More Than A Woman

She is a princess
Been treated like an apprentice
Plenty paper cuts on her heart
All patched up when I print this
Picture perfect
Mona Lisa with the smile
Poetic justice
Queen Latifah with the style
Living single
Due to independency
Can do bad on her own
Too strong to build chemistry
Really smart with her mouth
Well that never fails
Hammer on the head
That cracked with the nails
In dire need of a manicure
Just so, she can feel secure
Outside looking in
Man say it is insecure
Inside seeking out
She just wants a man to cure
Those wicked war wounds
Created by baboons

So many characters
Could have directed a cartoon
If you come with them games
Be willing to go overtime
If you are down to ride
Be prepared for overdrive
She is a trip
To the margins of Milky Way
Canvass of a cash cow
No gold-digger can milk away
Nurtures the Earth
Grants access to life
Sheltered since birth
With an attraction for light
So shine bright
Like a girl's best friend
Watch them read all about it
Like breaking news just in

Orgasm

Started at the bottom
Trying to build something from a doorway and a column
She cold as winter
But on these springs
I can make summer fall like it is autumn
To reach the climax
Quiet on the set
So I can paint the perfect picture
With a brush you can touch while wet
Why wait
Lie straight
Deep sea diving
No need for live bait
Impaired pleasure
Steady digging for hidden treasure
Invited islands
I hope you cleared your schedule
When we kiss
It is a bliss
Toes clinched
Tight as a fist
Domestic violence
Disturbing the peace
Domestic silence

We converge in the sheets
Sheesh
You still seem nervous to me
It is in my nature
To taste you
Do not worry about the feelings
Because you still numb from from the flavor
Turn off the lights
Slowly
I continue to soul seek
Go deep
Almost there
Goal reached
No gold medals or gold sheets
Your legs
So weak
Rock climbed a mountain
On my way to reach your peak

The Silent Treatment

Loud talking and complaining
Is another disease
Nevertheless, this is entertaining
Even over the seas
If every nation can understand violence
Then every language can comprehend silence
To bless my plate
I say my grace
Then eat off it
You speak your hate
I will not debate
Because you will feed off it
A blank response
Not even a laugh
No facial expressions
There is no need for mask
This is that concealed thrill
A hassle while bashful
Being booted by muted
Causing a quiet riot
Pleading peace treaty
We were never at war
Your words were mistreating
Therefore, I found the cure

Tattoos

I love the skin I am in
I hate those that stand for nothing
Pierced ink falls for something
Regardless the pain is coming
If I mark me up
I need a raincheck on sinning
What about the bumps and bruises from the beginning
I take these permanent scars
To the heart
Many times broken
But never apart
On my skin until the end
But when did this start
My unspoken stories
Of tragedies and glory
Not for entertainment
Ink is jewelry
Accessories for every single minute
This my life
Which is not about an image
The sky is not the limit
I will trade this shirt for a sleeve
These shades for a tear drop
When I lick that tramp stamp

You gone have to refill this pit stop
I should get a tatted wristwatch
Because I done wasted too much time
Trying get to get a chick hot
I am too cool
Tattooed ice cubes
Mean tats on a nice dude
Tats on my waist
When things get slight rude
Ink is reality
Please make the right move
Read the pages
Watch suffer turn to supper
Next time you will think twice before you judge a book by its cover

Wine And Weed

Natural components
Versus manufactured opponents
You can keep the antifreeze
And the beans with trampolines
All I need to balance beam
Is my fruits and plants
I am official
Not artificial
So when I draw the line
Do not draw your pistol
What I blow is loud
Without the whistle
I like it quiet
Autopilot when it go round
Silence them sirens when we come down
To each is own
Flashing lights tend to blow mine
No need to cosign
For cold wine
Because this here
Is all natural
Manmade is incompatible
Blended attitude with altitude
Put that on ice

Now that is radical
Who needs revenue for a stepping stool
Or an interview on a pedestal
Supply me a cup, lighter, and a parachute
Lights, camera, action
We gone be airing soon
Take off when I want
I am a walking air balloon

Never Give Up

These are spoken words
From a broken bird
One wing stiff
While the other still has the urge
To fight for another day on the Earth
And if I catch this wave
Let me surf
This food for thought
That I just served
Is a full course meal
Not hors d'oeures
Halfhearted finger foods
Can I please be excused
In need of fresh air
No inner tubes
Degraded and deflated
Still I cruise
Devastated never faded
Sunny blues
With tonic tunes
Like it is happy hour
Sonic boom
Hold your horses
And your suspenders

Even if you get backed down
Never surrender
Build yourself back up
Never surrender
A white flag with your name on it
The worst thing you could ever remember

Be Thankful

People will judge you from your outside
Before they get to know your inside
If we all were inside out
Those judges would not open their mouth
The world see them for who they are
You are scarred
The truth shall set you free
You are barred
Looking for light in the dark
It ought
To be a crime to look that good
With the appetite to starve
That kind of sounds like a curse, right
But when I seen her
It was love at first sight
Went from "oui" to "ahh"
And smooch for smooch
Now we at eye for an eye
And tooth for a tooth
Makes it hard to find my food
And when I finally do
It is hard to chew

Laugh it up
Right to my face
Countless ways to express my faith
No meal deal
Still said my grace

Most High

Given a vision
When I was at my most low
Blessed with the voice
To reach your untouched soul
Feet lifted
We all can walk on water
Labeled as legal aliens
Forced to cross that border
I refuse to let a man's law
Stand above god's words
You want a history lesson
Open the book of Proverbs
What is the Constitution
Compared to the Commandments
Imperfect rules
Used to command man
Led by lost souls
Our kids are abandon
Fellowship is the band-aid
Money is another mistake that man made
Leaving us socially strained
Physically drained
For a spiritual gain
On a scale

I am balanced to be mentally sane
Faith is dead without action
Sounds a lot like hope
Love is dead without passion
Looks like a lot smoke
The type you have to walk through
To see through
Exodus
The type of path you have to read through
Fine print
Could not undermine it
Taken out of context
As an advertised skit
Your soul was sold
Before it even sold out
Did not know the role
So you scored and rolled out
The red carpet to darkness
You reap what yow sow
Tarnished your harvest
Intentions of your people starving
I beg your pardon
We shall feast in Eden's garden

Been There Done That

I am in the lead by light years
In a league of my own
Shine bright through the nightmares
As I feed, off of the throne
Fight the current
To follow the clouds
Fear of a lonely future
So they follow the crowd
Run along with the wolf pack
Embrace me as the stand-alone lone wolf
Bragging over short films
That was originated from my long book
Knowledgeable oil leaking out my ink pen
Writing on the wall
Down the hall
Until it sinks in
Do not let your peers see the fear of you sinking
When peer pressure was the reason
Why you jumped off the deep end
Branded by bandits
Plans to see you panic
All the keys to open doors
But your access is not granted
Rejection is a universal horror

Life is a bitch
I still do adore her
Keep her rotting in the back like a spoiler
In my hood
It is first come first serve
Next serve left swerve
No nonsense from those with no nerves
Every aching moment
On edge
Cannot balance with bow legs
Every time somebody push
You gone beg
As soon as you give in
Outcome hatched eggs

24 Hours

Not enough time in a day
That is why I cannot blink
Not enough days in a week
That is why I cannot wink
Not enough weeks in a year
That is why I cannot sleep
Too many years in tears
That is why I cannot see
Too many words wounded
That is why I cannot speak
Too many trees uprooted
That is why I cannot think
Not enough blood in my tones
That is why I cannot drink
Not enough teeth in my homes
That is why I cannot eat
Not enough meat on my bones
That is why I cannot sink
Too many put in a box
That is why I cannot shrink
Too many invested in stock
That is why I cannot leave
Too many twisted, no locks
That is why we cannot link

On my P's and Q's
That is why they cannot scheme
Not enough weeks in a year
That is why they cannot dream
I am the mayor of the night
That is why they daydream

Letter From A Failure

Dear world,
I am the best thing that never happened
Every thought, word, and action
Were designated for dedication
Devastated the moment I reached my destination
Dusting feet on a farewell mat
Without stepping through the stairwell hatch
Disgusted by my inability to adjust to injustice
Rather dwell with the rubbish
Before my trust is abducted
Another law-abiding citizen being treated as a criminal
Punished for good deeds
Now that is a contradicting principle
Exit wombs will never heal with this damaged psyche
Devoted my love to get "the man" to like me
I am out raged just
All the necessities to be famous
No need for investments
When the vision is destined
Dimmed the light through the dark times
Claw grip on life with hawk eyes
Reason why the early bird got the worm
Because the night owl waits its turn
When it has the nerve

To take the dessert
It does not deserved
That owl has no choice
But to settle for a bird
Survival of the fittest
Product of our environment
What if I do not fit it
Forced into retirement
No words of encouragement
A couple of verbs
Wear and tear from corporate nourishment
Would not wish death upon anyone
However, exposure is a must
On a highway to hell
And guess who loaded the bus
Usual tour downtown
Not disturbed by disgust
Indeed, they entered clean
I need to intervene
Annoyed by the discuss
Fame is the worst thing that could have happened to me
Sailing at my own risk
Clever captain at sea
Taking a typical trounce for treasure
Salvation reduce to pleasure
Do whatever whenever
However to do better
Rewrote rules of the road
Demoted to new sailor
Setup to setback
Rather start from scratch like a true tailor
Cannot wait to get back on my feet
So they can step on my toes

Now I stride right
With each step for the sole
Tighten up your tongue
That is all I can tell you
Before I take a walk with success
I must crawl with the fist of failure

Printed in the United States
By Bookmasters